THIS JOURNAL BELONGS TO

Imprint: Independently published

www.ingramcontent.com/pod-product-compliance
Lightning Source LLC
Chambersburg PA
CBHW030705220526
45463CB00005B/1905
* 9 7 8 1 6 5 2 6 5 8 2 7 6 *